Journey with Jesus

Kara Mendez

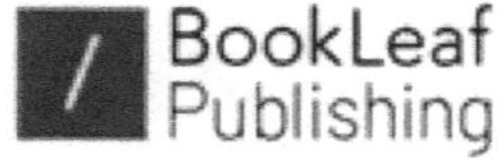

BookLeaf
Publishing

Presentation by *BookLeaf Publishing*

Web: www.bookleafpub.com

E-mail: info@bookleafpub.com

ISBN: 9789357210409

First edition 2022

DEDICATION

I would like to dedicate this book to my Lord and Savior, Jesus Christ, who has walked with me and led me on my incredible life journey in missions.

Additionally, I would like to dedicate this book to my loving husband, Mario, parents, David and Lori Denton, brother and sister-in-law, James and Anna Denton, my in-law's, Mario and Ingrid Mendez, my brothers and sisters-in-law in Guatemala, and countless family who have shown me their love and support.

ACKNOWLEDGEMENT

First and foremost, I would like to acknowledge my Heavenly Father for his amazing grace. Without Him, I could have never made it this far. I cannot imagine my life without the Lord.

Next, I would like to thank my wonderful, amazing husband that shares the same passion I have both in ministry and in life. Mario is my "half-orange" as they call it in Guatemala. He is my better half and I am so full of love and gratitude for all he does for me and our ministry. I love you, Marito.

Finally, I would also like to thank my incredible family: David and Lori Denton, James and Anna Denton, JP and Charlotte Foutch, Grandma Denton, Grandpa Denton who is now in heaven, Mario and Ingrid Mendez, Grandpa and Grandma Juarez, Grandpa Mendez, Grandma Mendez who is also now in heaven, all of my aunts, uncles, cousins both in the USA and in Guatemala, and all of my siblings-in-law. You all are the best! I love you all so much and I am incredibly blessed for the opportunity to have you in my life. I carry you in my heart wherever I am.

I also want to mention Ashley, Matt, Bethany, Stacy, Lauren, Leah, Mallory, Amanda, Paul, and Riley. You all hold a special place in my heart.

PREFACE

For many years, I have desired to express my faith and share it with the world. My life journey of faith in Jesus has been such a wild ride to say the least. All throughout the years, my father has been in ministry and my mother has always been such an amazing pastor's wife. They led such an amazing example of leadership and serving in ministry. Once my brother was born, we continued to be a beautiful family unit. They raised us in church and taught us to seek the will of God for our lives. I cannot imagine a life without the Jesus. My grandparents were also so influential growing up, teaching me to be generous and caring towards people around me.

It is to no surprise that I would be called to the mission field after so many impacting encounters with foreign missionaries and people so heavily involved in serving in ministry. With much passion, I finally began to write during the pandemic of 2020. These poems are a simple expression of how the Lord has done a work in my life and continues to do so on a daily basis. Once, I heard some say that Jesus has to come in and do heart surgery to cleanse us and transform us from the inside out. I thank God for this amazing journey He has taken me. Following Jesus has been the greatest journey in my life.

Puzzle Pieces

From the beginning
When God made me
His plan began to unravel
It's so easy to see

From Missouri to the Smoky Mountains
In beautiful Tennessee
My parents taught me to love Jesus
It was at four when I believed

Our neighbors from Honduras and
Church friends from other countries
God began to stir my heart
For many missionaries

I had always wanted to be a part
Of something greater than myself
If only I could go back and tell
That little girl to be more sure of herself

For the Lord had amazing plans
As she continued to grow
She learned about ministry and missions
Never knowing she was called to grow

All throughout her life

Striving to follow Jesus
It was God who always guided her
and placed all the puzzle pieces

Faith like a Mustard Seed

With each day that arrives
His mercies are anew
Opportunities are rising
Listen! He is calling you

The sun is brightly shining
There's no time to be afraid
Get up and get moving
It's time to seize the day

Each and every morning
Pray about your choice
Be prepared to follow Him
Listen for His gentle voice

As you feel the tug so strongly
Pulling on your heart
Discover what stirs inside
And that is where you start

Hard times will surely come
It's His strength that you will need
Your faith must grow and always be
Like the mustard seed

Off to GU

It came to choose a college
Since seventh grade I always knew
I packed up my belongings
Soon I was off to GU

I met incredible people
And even lived in the dorm
Now I had to make decisions
This was my new norm

After changing my majors
I didn't know what to do
For I was left with Spanish
And religion classes too

Through my time at Vespers
God began to stir my heart
For a hurting people
I knew He set me apart

To travel on three mission trips
He clearly spoke to me
Not really knowing my future
Then I could finally see

This experience at college
Truly impacted my life
After my Senior year
I became a wife

All because of my practicum
A special project had begun
God gave me the opportunity
to share about His Son

I will never forget my time at GU
My life is forever changed
May the name of Jesus always be known
And forever proclaimed

The Mountain View

Early in the morning
We could see the dew
On the grass and flowers
and on the plant leaves too

The air was fresh and
The sky was blue
God's mercies and love
Were always anew

With the gorgeous sunrise
The wind always blew
As we spent time with Jesus
Looking at the mountain view

Sweet Little Ones

In the beautiful mountains
Of a little, rural town
Lived lots of amazing people
With children all around

Gathering together
To learn about God's love
His mercy and forgiveness
And everything from above

They sat down beside the teacher
Until story time was done
How precious and so loving
Oh sweet little ones

Thankfulness

Lord, you are full of grace
You give us your mercy
I'm thankful for your kindness
And all you do for me

In the good times and bad
You are ever so near
I don't know what I'd do
If you were not here

You are my provider
You bestow us your care
Thank you Lord for everything
Especially for prayer

God Gave me You

Your love is so amazing
It is forever true
I'm eternally grateful
That God gave me you

Mi lindo esposo
Que puedo decir
Miles de palabras
Te quiero escribir

Thank you for your heart
And everything you do
To protect and care for me
Oh how I love you

Gracias por tu perdón
Y por siempre ser fiel
Tú eres muy guapo
Con un corazón de miel

God has truly blessed me
With a love I never knew
From now until eternity
God gave me you

Our Special Day

It was a beautiful, peaceful morning
The sun shining down on me
As I stood outside the ballroom
I gazed out on the balcony

It was an early December day
I just could not believe
That I was about to marry
My love's side I'd never leave

As I waited all dressed in white
I began to pray
And ask the Lord to speak to me
I listened to what He'd say

The love that you are feeling
Is how Jesus loves His bride
The church, the people so truly loved
He'll always be by your side

Such an whimsical moment
My husband took my breath away
I will never forget the remarkable love
We shared on our special day

You Need Only to be Still

When you find yourself
Anxiously searching for His will
Rest assured He has a perfect plan
You need only to be still

All throughout your life
Problems will arise
Seek the Lord in these moments
For He will hear your cries

In the moments of you fear and doubt
He will always fulfill
Each and every promise
You need only to be still

In the midst of pain or worry
When you don't know what to do
Ask Him for His guidance
It's Jesus you should pursue

When you feel like you cannot go on
As you're climbing up the hill
He's the one who fights for you
You need only to be still

He Loved the Children

There was a time on earth
When Jesus was here
To teach and heal
Where the people were near

Among the crown of people
Stood a group of little ones
Wanting to see Jesus
They began to approach the Son

The disciples stopped them
And told their parents no
That Jesus was too busy
It was time for them to go

When Jesus saw what happened
Clearly, he wasn't pleased
As He looked at the disciples
He said, "Let the children come to me."

Jesus loved the children
Closely He embraced them
In His arms, they were blessed and loved
For they belonged to Him

Humble Man

Humility displayed
Up on the cross
The ultimate sacrifice
That was the cost

He came to the earth
With a purpose and a plan
Giving us salvation
Oh humble man

The walk to the mount
With a crown of thorns in His head
Bearing the heavy cross
He carried it and lead

All the way to Calvary
Such pain to withstand
Maintaining such gentleness
Oh humble man

All we need

Have you ever wondered
What it is you truly need?
Turn your eyes to Heaven
Let Jesus take the lead

In a world fill of people pleasing
They will tell you what to do
Have all the latest shoes and clothes
Then wonder if this is really you

The fancy life is glamorous
With so much you can buy
The life that you are living
Maybe it is all a lie

All these things will not last forever
For you there's so much more
Peace, joy, contentment and love
He is at your heart's door

All you need is Jesus
In this crazy place we live
Turn your heart to God
There's nothing more that you can give

The Most Important Part of Christmas

Every year was special
Spent with family and friends
Each magical Christmas season
I never wanted it to end

My family taught me to be generous
To those who were in need
I loved to give so many gifts
The story of Jesus we would read

With my precious mother
We made lots of roll out cookies
With so many beautiful Christmas lights
We decorated our trees

Focusing on Jesus
And His miraculous birth
The most important part of Christmas
Because God sent His son to this earth

Jesus makes me fearless

In the midst of chaos
Each and every day
When I am scared
I take time to pray

Jesus makes me fearless

My hope comes from Jesus
This I can confidently say
For all He does for me
In His arms I will remain

Jesus makes me fearless

Because of His love
It makes me want to share
That God sent His son to die
And of the cross that He would bare

Jesus makes me fearless

Striving to follow Jesus
Daily seeking His face
As eternity awaits
I'm thankful for His grace

Jesus makes me fearless

Caring for me

One day I went outside
And I saw a tiny bird
I began to wonder
If my prayers were ever heard

I sat there quietly and
Watched the little bird
As it held bread in its mouth
I thought about my concerns

In my troubled heart
I began to pray
I softly spoke to Jesus
And knew exactly what to say

If you can provide for them
You can provide for me
I must trust in you
Whenever I'm in need

Each and every day
I will call out to you
It's a new opportunity
To see all that you will do

Thank you Lord Jesus
Now I can finally see
You are so incredibly good
You always care for me

Unexplainable Peace

Often in life
We feel insecure
It's peace we seek
This I am sure

Problems we'll face
But, we must take heart
For God who created us
Was here from the start

When danger arises
And we're overcome with fear
Worship, pray, and let Him speak
Jesus is always near

Unexplainable peace
Can always be found
Be still in His presence
Let His voice be renowned

Don't let you heart be troubled
In times when you're afraid
He'll give you courage and make you strong
Immense peace He'll give you along the way

I will wait on you

When faced with a decision
Real faith is a must
Not knowing the outcome
In Him we have to trust

All of my life
I never really knew
All of the moments
When I would need you

Sometimes life is great
But you never really know
It's during the tough times
We rely on you the most

In every circumstance
I know one thing is true
God, your plans are so perfect
I will learn to wait on you

Like a Butterfly

When we meet Jesus
There's so much we must know
We learn to pray and talk to Him
This is how it goes

Just like the process of a butterfly
There are stages we undergo
We must be changed and be transformed
In order for us to grow

Once we belong to Jesus
A new person we become
Our old life we leave behind
Then out new life has begun

We become a new creation in Christ
It's like having new wings to fly
We're on a new, beautiful journey
Just like a butterfly

Beautiful Little Girl

Once upon a time
In a simple home and town
Lived a beautiful little girl
Who wore a plastic crown

She had a tiny family of three
Who loved her very much
Daddy always made her laugh
Momma had the perfect touch

She loved to play with her dolls
And run around and sing
She loved to pray and go to church
And plan her future wedding

As she grew older
Her family began to move
Since her daddy was a pastor
She was used to the PK groove

There came a time within her heart
She wanted a forever friend
Maybe a little brother or sister
Oh when would God send?

This little girl was so happy
She just could not believe
Now she had a baby brother
What a heavenly gift she received

This beautiful little girl
A daughter of the King
She was blessed beyond measures
And thanked God for everything

Jesus makes me Worthy

Striving to be somebody
It's Jesus who makes me worthy

Since the day I gave my life
To my one and only King
Who came down from heaven
To Him I praise and sing

Striving to be somebody
It's Jesus who makes me worthy

Sometimes there are days
When I truly feel like a failure
But God faithfully walks with me
In Him I am secure

Striving to be somebody
It's Jesus who makes me worthy

Every day I must choose
To daily follow Jesus
He's the one who paid the price
For each and every one of us

I no longer have to strive

To be anyone other than me

It's Jesus who makes me worthy

Journey with Jesus

In all of my life
I never imagined
That God would use me
To impact the lives of many

Traveling to Guatemala
It's so incredible to know
That God can use one
If we are willing to go

Now as I grow older
My heart beats for people
My passion is my family
And the people in need

What an adventure it's been
Learning to grow and trust
As my husband and I continue to serve
On our journey with Jesus